D N

History, Heritage & Wildlife

Gavin McLean

University of Otago Press

Local Guide: Dunedin

Dedicated to Gail Birt and Clive Matthewson 'at Port'

Published by University of Otago Press
56 Union Street West, Dunedin, New Zealand
Fax: 64 3 479 8385. Email: university.press@stonebow.otago.ac.nz

First published 2003, ISBN 1 877276 41 3

Printed by Spectrum Print Ltd, Christchurch

Unless otherwise acknowledged, the photographs are by Gavin McLean.
The maps were created by Allan J. Kynaston.

Cover photographs
Front: The Clock Tower (1879), University of Otago.
Back, top: An old ship's anchor serves as a memorial at the Port Chalmers Lookout.
Back, bottom: St Clair beach.
Page 1: John Barr of Craigilee (1809–89) is one of the interesting residents of Dunedin's Northern Cemetery. A founder of the Burns Club, this Clutha farmer was famed for his poems and humorous verse: 'There's nae place like Otago yet, /There's nae wee beggar weans, /Or auld men shivering at our doors, /To beg for scraps or banes'.

Look for these Local Guides published by University of Otago Press:
Arrowtown, Dunedin, The Catlins, Oamaru, Stewart Island, Wanaka.
Futher titles are forthcoming, including: *Queenstown* and *Wellington.*

Contents

Driven around here

Left: First-year students listen to a mayoral welcome in the Octagon before going on to make their own entertainment.

Right: Portobello basks in the summer sunshine as summer fog builds up around Harbour Cone.

spent New Year here

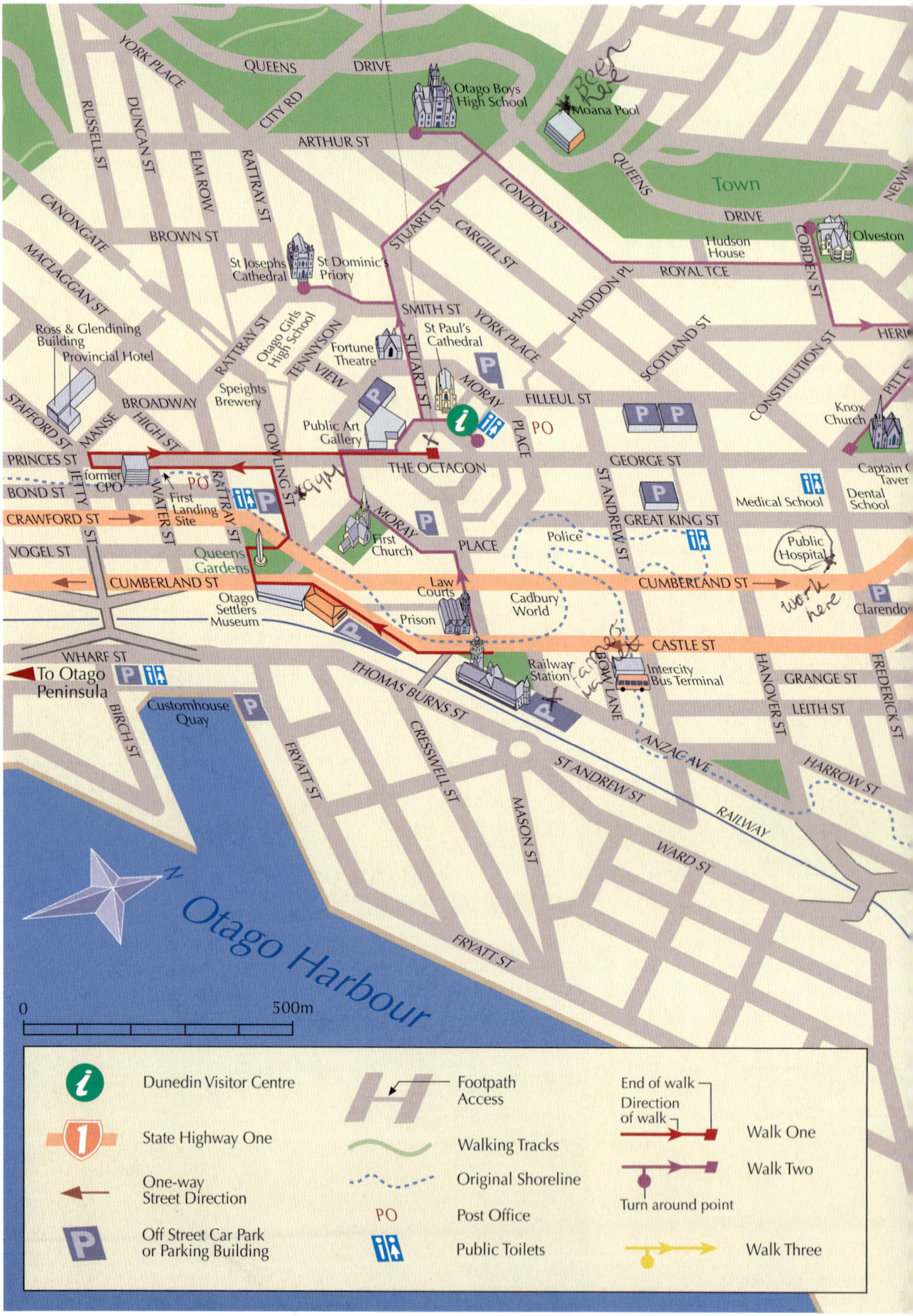

Dunedin City

had very nice coffee here. Regent is the theatre

The Octagon is a popular watering hole with tourists and locals alike.

1: A Short History

Go, trav'ler, unto others boast
of Venice and of Rome
Of saintly Mark's majestic pile
and Peter's lofty dome
Of Naples and her trellised bowers,
of Rhineland far away
These may be grand, but give to me
Dunedin from the Bay

So boasted Thomas Bracken, colonial New Zealand's unofficial poet laureate and creator of the national anthem, 'God Defend New Zealand' (first performed here in 1876). We will visit his grave on one of our walks, but love or hate his unfashionably sentimental verse, you have to admit that he was right.

There *is* something special about this city, one of the world's most southerly. Listen to the writers, filmmakers and musicians. In *Millennium*, historian Felipe Fernandez-Armesto described a city 'lined with spires and trimmed with towers, as heavy with human embellishments as an alderman's robes … a marvellous mirror, reflecting Victorian and Edwardian Britain from as far away as it is possible to get, through almost the whole length and density of the core and carapace of the earth'. In 1999, Robert Sarkies rolled 'Filmed on Location in Beautiful Dunedin' across the screen at the end of his movie *Scarfies*, a black comedy about the pothead denizens of a dank, dingy Dunedin student flat, very definitely the other side of the track from the first owners of Olveston or Larnach's Castle. From the cover of Matthew Bannister's book *Positively George Street*, band members face the camera at wintry St. Clair, four sets of chattering teeth hammering out the only 'Dunedin Sound' that day.

Number 49 Brown Street, just a short crawl from the brewery, starred in the movie Scarfies. *Damp? – sometimes – dirty? – yes, but Dunedin student flats have character!*

Left: Visitors make the most of the 1925–26 New Zealand and South Seas Exhibition on newly reclaimed Lake Logan: the modern Logan Park. With its 3.2 million visitors, it was Dunedin's greatest show. Note the Northern Cemetery on the hill.
The Press (Christchurch) Collection, Alexander Turnbull Library PAColl-3031

Scarfies, real or cinematic, symbolise Dunedin's seemingly endless capacity to accommodate both our more fiery political or artistic hell-raisers and some of the country's quietest old money. In 1998 George Griffiths called his musical tribute to Otago, 'From the Southern Marches'. A march, he explained, is a piece of music, but in old European terms it was also a border zone, a place of daring and danger. That is Dunedin. Not quite 'the last buffers before the Southern Ocean' as Fernandez-Armesto thought, but definitely a city that lives on the edge, environmentally, politically and economically, never quite sure whether it wants to be a commercial powerhouse or a spiritual or ecological 'City on the Hill'.

Dunedin from Bell Hill in the 1850s. A couple of small trading vessels lie alongside 'Wickliffe Pier', the first little jetty running out from the landing place, approximately near the modern Exchange. The mudflats were a curse. G Lamond Collection, Alexander Turnbull Library F-38710-1/2-

'MUD-EDIN'

Modern Otago began in 1848 as the Free Church of Scotland's take on the 'Wakefield' organised settlement. Here the Otago Association wanted to create a godlier, more socially homogeneous society. Captain William Cargill and the stern, humourless, Rev. Thomas Burns dreamed of a Free Church, small-farmer society with morals as straight as its fence lines and hedgerows. That was wishful thinking, for the province was no tabula rasa. For a start, a small Maori population, Kai Tahu/Kati Mamoe, occupied a sparse string of predominantly coastal sites. Kati Mamoe had been there since the sixteenth century, moving in alongside the earlier people known as Waitaha. In the seventeenth and eighteenth century fresh invaders, Kai Tahu from the eastern North Island, moved down, largely assimilating Kati Mamoe. Numbers were never big – the kumara needed to sustain large populations would not grow south of Banks Peninsula – and people lived a predominantly hunter-gatherer lifestyle.

For several decades sealers and whalers had also been operating along the southern coastline, supplemented more recently by wealthier settlers anticipating the arrival of systematic colonisation: men like Johnny Jones near Waikouaiti, whose produce helped feed infant Dunedin, but his sheep also undermined the Otago Association's plans for concentrated, socially ordered settlements. So, too, would later passenger lists, being neither as godly nor select as the elect would have liked. As with any nineteenth-century frontier society, it was a bit of a free-for-all. And rough. K.C. McDonald described late 1850s Dunedin as 'a depressing little huddle of primitive buildings in a muddy hollow. Houses and shops alike were almost all of wood, often unpainted, with warping weatherboards and moss-grown shingles'. Streams flowed down Maclaggan and London streets. Every downpour showed why the wags called Dunedin 'Mud-edin'.

Goldrush Dunedin in 1861. Princes Street is still a daunting sea of mud and the little coasters still lie on their side in the background at low tide, but masonry buildings are starting to appear alongside timber structures. Alexander Turnbull Library G-8370-1/1-

Local Names

Dunedin takes its name from the old Gaelic word for Edinburgh. For a while it looked like the town might be saddled with that clumsy colonial standby, a European city name prefixed by the word 'New' ('New Edinburgh' in this case until publisher William Chambers suggested the shorter, sweeter name in 1843. Port Chalmers is named after Dr Thomas Chalmers, the Free Church leader and one of nineteenth-century Scotland's most influential citizens.

Last century there was some controversy about the correct Maori name for the province. Some favoured Otakou, but scholars now agree that the early Europeans heard aright when they wrote down the southern dialect (which often voices the 'k' as 'g') as Otago. Otepoti is Dunedin's Maori name. Port Chalmers's Maori name is often given as 'Koputai', and the much reclaimed, dredged and otherwise despoiled bay still goes by that name. See two Otago Heritage Books publications by George Griffiths, *Names and Places in Southern New Zealand* (1990) and *The Spurious Maori Placenames of Southern New Zealand* (2002) for more on local names.

Getting around was the bane of everyone's life. Ships came no closer than Port Chalmers. From there, everyone and everything had to be offloaded into small craft and taken up the narrow, shallow harbour channels to the Dunedin waterfront, where a rickety jetty sat high and dry at high tide. More often than not, newcomers had to wade ashore across extensive mudflats to reach what we now call the Exchange. Dry land was little better. Bell Hill's rocky, bush-clad bulk effectively split Princes Street in two, preventing wheeled vehicles from running between the Exchange and the Octagon and making 'a stiff climb even for pedestrians'.

But all that was about to change.

Above: When this photograph was taken about 1860 from Canongate, Bell Hill (left) still cut the Exchange area off from the rest of the township. *Alexander Turnbull Library F-4372-1/2-*

NEW ZEALAND'S BIGGEST CITY

Dunedin took off after 1861, when Gabriel Read famously found payable quantities of gold 'shining like the stars in Orion on a dark frosty night'. It took a while for the penny to drop, but by December 14,000 people – seven times Dunedin's pre-rush population – were staked out on the Tuapeka and Waipori fields. The town almost emptied out before new waves of fortune-seekers rushed in. 'Greatness is forced upon us', the *Otago Witness* declared. Otago's population soared by eighty per cent between 1861 and 1864, when Dunedin's 20,000 inhabitants made it New Zealand's largest city. It remained top dog for another seventeen years.

In an era that believed in progress with religious fervour, only the disgruntled Free Church founders worried about this growth. Although their dogma of class settlement, low wages, 'sufficient price' and 'concentration' had been faltering long before gold, hardliners lashed back, most famously when Edward Bowes Cargill rashly hoped that 'notwithstanding the great influx of rogues and vagabonds, settlers should preserve their 'Old Identity'. Smug Scots Presbyterian jibes at the 'New Iniquity' – the mainly Australian newcomers – provided fodder for balladeer 'The Inimitable' Charles Thatcher, best remembered for his witty hit, 'The Old Identity'.

The song took off as the diggers baited the Scots, adding insult to indigestion by labelling that coarse mainstay of the boarding house table, the barracouta, 'the Old Identity'. Swamped and ridiculed, the Free Church hardliners retreated. Some diehards fought hymns and music at kirk services, but most went with the cash flow. Cargill quickly made his peace (and his money) with the 'New Iniquity'.

The city transformed itself almost overnight. Down, thanks as much to sweated prison labour as to political vision, came Bell Hill, its hefty scalp feeding the reclamations that pushed the city fringe out over the mudflats to deeper water. Elsewhere, tall masonry buildings thrust up, many of which we shall admire on our walks. Local government took over from ad hocery. A new Dunedin City Council replaced the old Town Board in 1865 amidst much mud-slinging, the Otago Harbour Board appeared in 1874, and a gaggle of borough councils ringed the city core.

But it was not all wealth and progress. Goldrush Dunedin was definitely a rough, tough, disease-ridden place, especially around 'The Devil's Half Acre' around Walker Street (modern Carroll Street). There people like Barbara Weldon, who came to Dunedin in 1863 and became 'the most drunken and disorderly woman in Dunedin', made her living on the game here until 1869, when they literally ran her out of town by putting her on the coach to Hokitika.

While many scratched a pathetic earning from the city's rough streets, others prospered. It is important to remember, as historian Jim McAloon cautions, that by imperial standards, Dunedin's wealthy, the colony's richest, were still hands-on entrepreneurs. *No Idle Rich*, indeed. In Dunedin they launched enterprises that mushroomed into national players. These included stock and station agents Wright Stephenson & Co., music dealers Charles Begg & Co., coffee merchants W. Gregg & Co., cordial manufacturers Lane's Ltd, engineers A. & T. Burt, drapers and woollen millers Ross & Glendining, ironmongers A. Briscoe & Co. and John Edmond Ltd., merchants Neill & Co., publisher H. Wise & Co., carriers NZ Express Co., soap manufacturers McLeod Bros and others. Commerce such as this enabled the city to build a Raj-style building in Great King Street in 1865 to house the New Zealand Exhibition, our first, which was visited by 31,250 people a mere seventeen years after the *John Wickliffe* and the *Philip Laing* had dropped anchor off Port Chalmers.

The Old Identity

'Go on in the old fashion
And ne'er improve the town
And still on all new comers,
Keep up a fearful 'down'
Don't alter your Post Office–
Let that old Jetty be–
And thus you'll be preserving
The Old Identity'

Charles Thatcher

Rock solid. This little bit of Burlington Street hints at how difficult Bell Hill must have been to demolish.

By 1870 Princes Street had been transformed. The footpaths and the road have been upgraded and the buildings, mainly banks (the Bank of Otago is the three-storey building on the left), have taken on a solid, permanent air. The building on the right with the distinctive tower is the 1868 post office. The university took it over in 1877 and the Colonial Bank six years later. From1900 it was the stock exchange.
Alexander Turnbull Library F-4505-1/1-

The 1870s launched manufacturers Shacklocks and Mosgiel Woollens, Standard Insurance, National Insurance and the Colonial Bank. In 1873 Bendix Hallenstein started his long-lived clothing chain; he later backed another national retailer, the DIC. Along Water Street out on the reclamation you could find the Westport Coal Company, the big pastoral firm NMA and the colossal Union Steam Ship Company. Dunedin and Scottish capitalists formed Union Steam in 1875, directed by the colonial-born James Mills, son of a customs waiter. Mills made it to Otago in 1849, early enough to impress Johnny Jones. Within a year Union took over its main coastal competitor and in 1878 it dominated the Tasman by acquiring its chief Australian rival. It just kept on growing and by 1883, when its new headquarters was being finished, it was sewing up the coal trade. Architect David Ross gave Mills an impressive Italian-style pile, the roofline a riot of minarets, ironwork and flagpoles, dominated by the observatory dome, from which company managers watched ships coming up the harbour. The centre of the façade, surmounted by 'a pyrament with an emblematic design (globe, anchor, cable etc) enclosing a clock', symbolised the ambition and reach of Mills and of the Dunedin business community.

But poverty still stalked city streets, within walking distance of the Union Company's offices or the Royal Terrace dress circle. The Long Depression of the 1880s and early 1890s hit hard. Slum conditions were common around Maclaggan Street, today's student quarter and 'The Flat', the crowded streets of South Dunedin. Here conditions worsened as employment fell and factory owners tightened their workers' belts. On 30 September 1888 the Rev. Rutherford Waddell from St Andrew's Church preached 'the most influential sermon in New Zealand history'. It denounced 'the sin of cheapness', the cost-cutting by manu-

Iona Church dominates this David De Maus ca 1883s view out over Port Chalmers's busy wharves. Immigrant ships and wool ships lie alongside the old Export Wharf (right), hulks are in the centre and the Union Company's trans-Tasman flier Rotomahana *is departing.*
D A De Maus Collection, Alexander Turnbull Library G-2564-1/1-

facturers and middlemen that was creating 'sweated' labour. Dunedin women and boys in the garment and footwear trades put in 72-hour weeks in dirty, dangerous plants for nine shillings. Outworkers fared even worse. Waddell's exposé inspired the *Otago Daily Times* to investigate. Soon the paper was shaming conservative politicians to act humanely. Late Victorian Dunedin was a political and trade union powerhouse and battleground.

It was also still one of the four main centres. A hundred years ago New Zealanders could talk meaningfully about four of them. Auckland led at 67,226, and Dunedin had slipped behind Christchurch's 57,041, but at 52,390, the city and suburbs were just ahead of Wellington's mushrooming 49,344. But there was little to separate the four and Dunedin made up for its relative decline by remaining the commercial and industrial capital of New Zealand. And electric trams and other new inventions added a touch of modernity to New Zealand's cosmopolitan capital, with its Chinese and Lebanese minorities.

The northern centres, benefiting from the opening up of the North Island interior and from dairy farming, also cashed in on the opening of the Panama Canal in 1914. This drained trade away from the old southern ocean routes that had seen ships touch Bluff and Dunedin first. The new route for the 'Home boats' also altered the old trans-Tasman trade routes. Little wonder then, that the Union Company, flogged off unwisely by Mills to P&O in 1917, moved its head office to Wellington in 1921. That was the biggest blow in a seemingly unending drift north.

At first the city weathered this adversity fairly well. So many national head offices had established themselves here in late Victorian times that they provided a cushion for many decades. In 1925–6 Dunedin staged its last hurrah, its third international exhibition since 1865. Not even Wellington in 1939–40 exceeded

Dunedin's attendances of 3.2 million over twenty-four weeks, all held at the specially reclaimed Logan Park. But after that, and despite the pleasantries of the 1948 centennial celebrations, it was all downhill, albeit made less painful by the fact that the city was at least sinking on an even keel.

Our Walks and Drives

Three walks, two drives and a selection of highlights take you around most of central Dunedin's historical, architectural and ecotourism landmarks. The first walk takes in the city's old landing site, reclamations and commercial heart. The second walk showcases the city's public buildings and places, and the homes of its Victorian/ Edwardian wealthy. The third walk highlights the university area and the Gardens. But in a city with so many attractions, this book has to be selective. For more on the city's geology, flora and fauna, see the University of Otago Press's *Wild Dunedin* by Neville Peat and Brian Patrick. The guidebooks listed on page 64 detail its historical and architectural heritage. Visit or email the Visitor Centre in the Octagon for pamphlets on walks and tours, advice on opening hours and to make the prior bookings that many places require (visitor.centre@dcc.govt.nz).

Finally, some of the farm or bush walks can be closed during Spring lambing season or for forestry maintenance. Ask the Visitor Centre.

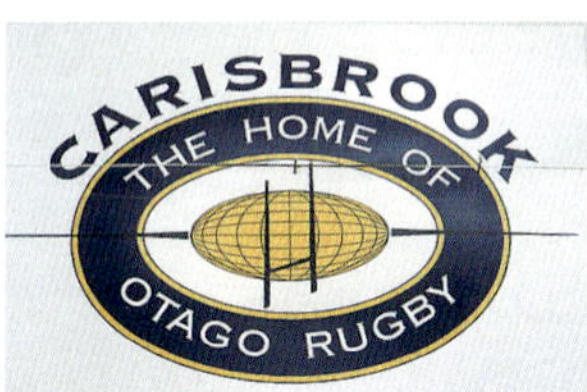

JUST THE OTHER DAY

The collapse of Mosgiel Limited in 1979 symbolised the loss of manufacturing, although many may have felt more keenly the end of the bottling of Speight's in the city a few years later. The economic upheavals of the 1980s brought more changes: trimmed government services, local authority restructuring and the loss of some of the few remaining big national head offices, National Insurance and Hallensteins.

But Dunedin was not dead. That smokestack era giant, the Hillside Railway Workshops, shed jobs but survived, and the city made the most of Port Chalmers's container port status. The port company and 'Port' residents have not always seen eye-to-eye, but boxes, logs and woodchips come and go in increasing quantities. The city has also benefited from the new deepwater fishing industry, which now dominates shipping movements in the Upper Harbour. Late last century Dunedin pushed its boundaries out in all directions to swallow up Mosgiel, Waikouaiti and other communities over the hill. That sleight of hand made it New Zealand's largest city geographically, stretching 125km along the coastline from Taieri Mouth in the south to Pleasant River in the north. Demographically, however, Hamilton overtook it in the population stakes.

Nevertheless, some big factories remain, smaller businesses such as computer graphics firms have taken root, and the big tertiary sector, feeding 20,000 or more students though the degree and diploma mills, keeps many well-paid jobs in the city. As we shall see on our walks, drives and tours, heritage and ecotourism have also perked up things, spawning nests of café tables in George Street and the Octagon. Sure, there has been a little artful tweaking here and there. Carisbrook's 'House of Pain' has been glitzed up like a suburban mall. The Otago student has morphed into the Scarfie. While you are more likely to see a moa than anyone resembling the brewery's 'Southern Man' stereotype in George Street, you will also see that at heart Dunedin's natural attractions, heritage and culture remain robustly and distinctively authentic.

Above: *'Gingerbread George' Troup's magnificent railway station is still an eye-catcher. Edwardian pride in the iron road extends even to the tiled floor of the foyer (opposite).*

Below: *Every Saturday a growers' market is held at the Railway Station northern carpark. It's a great place to find local produce, including organic products.*
Robin Frame

Go here regularly as it is cheaper than supermarket & the produce is much fresher. Very fresh fish!

2: Queen's Gardens / Exchange Walk

Our walk begins at one of the world's great railway stations. The fact that only the Taieri Gorge Railway's excursion train still uses it takes nothing away from the sheer magnificence of 'Gingerbread George' Troup's 1906 railway station. Exuberant in its Marseilles tiles, Central Otago basalt, Oamaru stone and Aberdeen granite, Dunedin's station oozes Edwardian confidence in a system at its apogee. Once New Zealand's busiest station, Dunedin declined from the 1970s as suburban services and branch lines closed. Fortunately the council bought Troup's triumph in 1994 for restoration. It remains a transport hub, used by buses and by the tourist trains. It also houses the Cleveland Living Arts Centre and other tenants. Do not miss the magnificent tiled booking office and first floor vestibule, a riot of tiles, stained glass and decorative ironwork.

Taieri Gorge Railway

One of Dunedin's more successful tourist ventures began modestly in the late 1970s, when Otago Railway and Locomotive Society stalwarts formed the Otago Excursion Train Trust to fill the gap after the state railways stopped running excursion trains. Since then its carriages, old and new, have travelled to just about everywhere on the rail network. In 1987 the Trust started running carriages over the scenic Taieri Gorge line, a venture that survived even the closure of the railway, for the Dunedin City Council bought the track from Taieri to Middlemarch and joined forces with the Trust to create the Taieri Gorge Railway Ltd. The joint venture now runs daily trips and maintains 60km of track through some of the country's most rugged scenery.

Planning to go on this soon

Walk south along Anzac Avenue's footpath. Across the road are the Law Courts (see page 22), which we shall inspect on our next walk. Just south is the old Dunedin Prison, a suitably forbidding-looking red-brick pile from 1896 that is said to owe something to the influence of London's New Scotland Yard. For most of its life the old slammer also doubled as a police station. Above it, the rear of First Church hints at how Bell Hill once divided the two hearts of early colonial Dunedin.

But we are not quite finished with trains. Two preserved steam locomotives form the advance guard of our next stop, the Otago Settlers' Museum. The smaller, all brass, iron and whistles, is 'Josephine', one of just five surviving double-ended Fairlies in the world. It first ran between Dunedin and Port Chalmers in 1872 and worked until 1916. The big black JA 1274 is a later (1956) beast, the last steam locomotive built by the city's Hillside Railway Workshops. That is fitting, for this site of a former railway station. The museum has an interesting history. The Otago Early Settlers' Association, as it was then known, was formed in 1898 to commemorate the province's fiftieth jubilee. The museum's display policy has moved with the times. These days it also showcases Kai Tahu, Chinese and other social history, but the Smith Gallery still crowds the wall with portraits of those stern-faced Victorian patriarchs and matriarchs that were the Settlers' mainstay. The museum's southern end now houses carts, cars and trams in that art deco gem, the old 1939 New Zealand Railways Road Services Passenger Station, which retains its heritage features, right down to the booking hall and deco lettering. The museum is open daily, except for Good Friday and Christmas Day.

Cross Anzac Avenue to Queen's Gardens. Through its leafy fringe the elegant buildings, hotels, insurance companies and the like remind us that this was the place to be when ships brought people up to the Steamer Basin, and when the trains stopped nearby. Queen's Gardens started as the Triangle, a bare patch of unkempt land after the station and rail yards pulled out. After some debate it was declared a reserve and the Amenities Society planted and fenced it. In 1889 businessman Wolff Harris added a touch of class with the fountain that now plays in the Botanic Gardens. Its replacement was the eight-sided stone Cenotaph, which still stands tall and proud. The city trimmed some of architect William Gummer's decorative work, but his 27-metre tower still inspires. The Duke of York unveiled it on 17 March 1927. Nearby is the statue of Queen Victoria, which has been frowning regally and imperially out across the street to the appropriately named Imperial Building on the corner of Lower High and Dowling Streets since 1901. Its presence inspired Dunedin to rename the Triangle Queen's Gardens in 1904 (the official name, Victoria Gardens, never caught on). Just southwest of her, isolated by the modern traffic, is a statue of Dr D.M Stuart, his back more or less turned to the city. We will encounter a fine bust of him outside Knox Church (page 30).

From the northern end of Queen's Gardens cross into Dowling Street, to leave behind the reclaimed land and tackle a tamed remnant of Bell Hill. As the buildings suggest, this is one of the city's more historic streets. Imperial Buildings is on the left. On your right there are several interesting buildings. The quirkiest is the old Garrison Hall, built by public subscription for the Volunteers and opened by the governor in 1879. Its exuberant battlements and pediments were butchered long ago, but the huge lion and the unicorn above the door still delight. For many years it has been the home of film and television production in Dunedin. Milford House was the headquarters of Hallenstein Brothers, or

Opposite top: Part of the old Dunedin prison.

The Cenotaph. William Gummer's eight-sided column soars above the trees, fittingly for a structure designed to be seen above the heads of the crowd on Anzac and Armistice Days.

Opposite centre: Kiwi and raupo, symbols of New Zealand identity, adorned the museum building when it opened as a small extension to the art gallery.

Opposite bottom: 'Josephine', Otago's pioneering double-ended Fairlie engine, has not raised steam for decades but it is a key Settlers' Museum attraction.

The sovereign's motto Dieu et Mon Droit ('God and My Right') and the imperial lion and unicorn point to the former Garrison Hall's patriotic origins.

'HB', as most called it, from 1883 until 1988. HB began in 1873 when Bendix Hallenstein established the New Zealand Clothing Factory to supply his stores, of which there were over thirty by 1900. Designed by David Ross, Hallenstein's pride and joy is built of plastered triple brick on a Port Chalmers breccia base. Apart from ground floor offices, the entire building was used for garment manufacturing and warehousing, employing 300 workers. An opponent of sweated labour, Hallenstein once declared that he 'would prefer to abandon our business rather than carry it on, if it can only be remunerative by starvation wages'.

Across Princes Street the grey bulk of the Dowling Street steps (built last century to replace earlier ones) rears up, another legacy of the assault on Bell Hill. Near them are the Excelsior Apartments, formerly the Oriental Hotel. An earlier Oriental would have looked at home on the set of 'Lord of the Rings', as it was a spiky grotesque that seemed to rise out of the blasted rock.

Walk south along Princes Street's left footpath past an eclectic mix of modern buildings and Victorian survivors, most looking a little down-at-heel, victims of the postwar drift north along George Street. A hundred years ago, though, it was a different story, as two former bank buildings near the High Street intersection show. The National Bank of 1913 still impresses with its distinctive dark cladding of Australian trachyte and sandstone. The former Bank of New Zealand building at the intersection is an 1879 wonder, revered for its ornate banking chamber ceiling. But it is merely the top layer of a wonderfully historic site. Here an early hotel, the Royal, lit the way to the old Dunedin waterfront over 150 years ago. In 1862 the BNZ built a two-storey masonry building here. That was better than you would have found in most northern cities, but goldrush Dunedin's booming economy quickly left it behind. Down it came after just seventeen years, to be replaced by W.B. Armson's magnificent pile. In 2001–2 it was the courthouse while the Law Courts were being conserved.

Monuments are fighting a losing battle with traffic in this part of town. Built in the Octagon in 1864, the Cargill Monument soon went south to the Exchange, or Customhouse Square, as they then called this part of the world (the word 'Exchange' has slipped and colonised the entire area). Said to have been influenced by Edinburgh's memorial to Sir Walter Scott, provincial engineer Charles Sawyer's monument is an exuberant Gothic riot of spikes and spires, although Victorian Dunedinites thought it 'too wedding cake' for their taste. Behind the monument you will see the top storeys of Consultancy House in Bond Street, best known as the New Zealand Express Company building. Believe it or not, this was Dunedin's first Chicago-style 'skyscraper': nothing Auckland, Wellington or Christchurch had matched when it opened in 1910.

Top: When completed in 1911, the Princes Street branch of the National Bank was one of the city's last classical masonry buildings.

Centre: The detailing around the Princes Street door to the former Bank of New Zealand building is exquisite. The building is made from a familiar mix of Port Chalmers bluestone and Oamaru stone.

Cargill's Monument has sat in the Exchange since 1872. In the background are Consultancy House (1910, ex New Zealand Express Company building) and John Wickliffe House (1977).

We are now in the heart of the Exchange. The name comes from the old Stock Exchange (built as the post office, then used by the university and by the Colonial Bank), which once ruled the roost here. The city foolishly allowed that fine old building to come down more than thirty years ago. Much earlier this was the muddy landing area for early colonial Dunedin. Stroll along Princes Street and duck a few metres down the Water Street side of John Wickliffe House, where a plaque in the footpath shows where the first settlers from the *John Wickliffe* stepped ashore in 1848.

This plaque in Water Street marks the old landing site.

Continue south along Princes Street past the interwar former Dunedin Chief Post Office, whose rear is adjacent to a controversial canoe landing site once granted but never given to local Maori. Wellington had usurped Dunedin's role as New Zealand's financial capital when it opened, but its impressive dimensions and those of the former T&G Building (next block, just past Lawson's classical former Bank of Otago building) show that the city still punched above its weight.

From this corner, look up Stafford Street to the second building on the right. The Provincial Hotel once extended all the way to Princes Street and was THE Dunedin goldrush hotel. Cobb & Co. coaches ran from here to Gabriel's Gully and publican Shadrack Jones is considered New Zealand's first real impresario. Its tall neighbour, the Ross and Glendining Building, once housed a branch of that big firm's manufacturing business.

Walk north along the western side of Princes Street. Now owned by a chain, the former Wain's Hotel, gutted internally, is a riot of gargoyles, including Neptune and his daughters Pelias and Neleus. As you walk north to return to the Octagon and coffee, you will pass Louis Boldini's Grand Hotel, part of the Southern Cross Hotel complex on the corner of Princes and High Streets. When it opened in 1883, 6000 people traipsed through simply to admire its magnificence, which included a new-fangled electric lift. The roof has lost some of its splendour, but there are enough carved figures on the façade to compensate.

That completes our first walk.

The Exchange remained Dunedin's commercial heart until the 1950s. Thus the former Dunedin Chief Post Office was finished in 1936, to overshadow Robert Lawson's classical ANZ (ex Union) Bank of 1874.

Below: In its heyday the Provincial stretched all the way to Princes Street. This was the heart of early goldrush Dunedin, the base for impresario Shadrack Jones.

Sea gods stare out from the facade of Wain's Hotel.

City Centre

3: Stuart Street / City Rise Walk

Our second walk begins almost in the shadow of the railway station that helped make this one of Dunedin's grandest streets early last century. But the slightly earlier (1902) Law Courts, with a marble statue of justice set high on the façade, need not feel inferior. Built from that popular Dunedin combination of Port Chalmers breccia and Oamaru stone to Government Architect John Campbell's design, it is a Gothic triumph, now restored after lengthy bureaucratic dillydallying.

A bit further up Stuart Street on the right are the brick offices of the *Otago Daily Times*, New Zealand's first daily newspaper (1861). When men like businessman/politician Sir Julius Vogel or George Fenwick (who crusaded against the clothing trade 'sweating' scandals in the late 1880s) edited it, the *ODT* was a force in the land. But it is something of a cuckoo in this nest, built for the defunct *Evening Star*. It has what must be New Zealand's smallest and slowest lift, the closest you can get to premature burial.

Cross to the left footpath to the Law Courts Establishment, once the Auld Scotland Hotel. Known as the Law Courts since 1902, it was rebuilt in the 1930s and was fifty years ago still good enough for the Queen. Continue up to Moray Place, which literally runs rings around the Octagon. The large building on the corner with Moray is the Security Buildings (1917), one of James Fletcher's early jobs. It earned its place in history on 5 February 1962 when solicitor James Ward died after opening a parcel bomb. No one knows who did it. For many years they kept his name on his old office window as a mark of respect. Around the windowsill at the Moray Place end there is another curiosity: round pockmarks created with coins by children queuing to enter the old swimming baths.

Left: The marble statue of Justice in the Law Courts' tower (centre front) was imported from Italy.

Above: The Security Buildings are closely associated with building empire founder James Fletcher.

Right: Traces left by children's pennies as they queued to enter the swimming pool and carved into the soft Oamaru stone.

Follow Moray Place to First Church, arguably New Zealand's finest nineteenth-century building. The memorial to the Rev. Thomas Burns inside the door is fitting, because First Church was his pet project. Burns had to wait a decade for the provincial government to lop twelve metres from Bell Hill and relocate or demolish fifty buildings, Burns's new manse included. On 15 May 1868 he finally laid the foundation stone for a building he would not live to see completed. A turret blew down in 1872 and the spire, built too short, had to be dismantled and rebuilt, but First Church has been a landmark since 1873. Architect Robert Lawson gave Burns his 'ornament to the town of Dunedin', that, needless to say, some 'Scotch Kirk' members thought too fancy. In 1885 dissidents formed a breakaway church when hymn singing was added to services.

Continue along Moray Place and follow the footpath on the west side of Princes Street up to the Octagon. The glorious pile on the corner is the Haynes Building, built in 1914 and extended in the early 1920s. In the days of trams and single-income households its Savoy Restaurant attracted the afternoon tea set. Our walk also takes us past the old DIC – Drapery and General Importing Company – department store, once a household name, with branches in many cities. Since 1996 the building has housed the Dunedin City Art Gallery. Founded in 1884 by William Hodgkins, Dunedin's gallery is New Zealand's oldest, and one of its best. The main entrance is in the Octagon. The galleries feature modern art and touring exhibitions, but also plenty of the works that appealed to Dunedin's wealthy Victorians – works by Turner, Gainsborough, Machiavelli, Monet, Tissot and Claude Lorrain and others. Admission is free.

First Church is an Oamaru stone Gothic treasure.

Dunedin has one of the country's most impressive art galleries. The Ciema is next door to here on the octagon.

The old DIC in Princes Street was once one of the city's largest department stores.

Went to a wedding here

The Octagon deserves a book of its own. Ever since Charles Kettle laid out an octagonal reserve in the centre of the Moray Place 'square', controversy has raged about its use and appearance. Much of what you see dates from the 1990s, when in came the covered walkways, poles and banners and out went the kitschy 'dancing' Star Fountain (1966) – Engelbert Humperdinck with water jets. The Octagon was fairly isolated until the Princes Street cutting went through Bell Hill and was derelict for many years, briefly housing the Cargill Monument. By then the road had gone through the centre despite protests. But the Octagon was still 'a standing disgrace to the community, an eyesore to most of the citizens, and an object of ridicule to strangers' when it gained its star attraction, the statue of poet Robert Burns, the Rev. Thomas Burns's uncle. Refurbished recently, 'Robbie' has sat there since his unveiling on 28 March 1887. Pavement plaques honour Dunedin literary greats.

The buildings facing the Octagon are a typically Kiwi frontier mixture of the good, the bad and the ugly. We shall focus on two of the four corners. In the southeast corner the Regent Theatre sits atop a site with a past more chequered than most. In December 1879 a hotel burned down here, killing twelve people. The façade you see belonged to the rebuilt hotel, which became a movie theatre in 1927–8. Falling cinema attendance in the television era almost killed the Regent until a local trust rescued it thirty years ago. Since then the show has been on the road for Dunedin's largest live entertainment venue.

From his perch in the Octagon, 'Robbie' poses for the cameras.

St Paul's Cathedral from Municipal Lane, showing the 1971 chancel.

The northwest corner of the Octagon is full of interesting places. Right on the George Street intersection is one of the city's finer modern structures, the Civic Centre. You can walk through this to another competently executed modern building, the Dunedin Public Library. It has a well-stocked New Zealand Room and also houses the McNab New Zealand Room Collection and the Reed Rare Books Collection, gifted by the famous publisher and author, who lived in the city for much of his life. Beside the library is the old Town Hall, designed by Robert Lawson in 1880. After 1963 it sported an undignified metal 'cap', the result of earthquake jitters, but in 1994 the city reinstated the old stairs up from the street and rebuilt its crowning glory, the tower, in modern, quake-resistant materials. It houses the Visitor Centre and is the pick-up point for many of the tours.

The spiky, greying Gothic Revival church on the corner, St Paul's Cathedral, dates from 1919 and was designed by Edmund Sedding for the Anglican Church. Take the magnificent flight of Takaka Marble steps up (thirty-eight to be precise) and look inside. Gothic met Visigoth about thirty years ago. The cathedral's rear section, the chancel, completed in 1971, is by architect Ted McCoy in uncompromising modern style. Some have praised McCoy's courage. Others compare his addition to the sagging rear end of a pantomime donkey. You decide.

Restaurants and small retailers now call the Stuart Street terrace houses home.

A former church, the Fortune is one of the city's premier theatres.

Cross to the south side of Upper Stuart Street. On your left you will pass the handsome terrace townhouses built for Herbert Haynes just over a century ago. Dunedin has several terraces but these are the grandest, with plaster facades and balconies, all designed to impress middle-class professionals and city-dwellers. But not their servants. A Historic Places Trust assessment describes their kitchens as 'dark and sunless, and the servants' bedroom, as in many old Dunedin houses was minuscule'. The handsome church building on the Moray Place intersection is the Fortune Theatre. Robert Lawson designed it as the Wesleyan (later Trinity Methodist) Church and the building served its congregations until the 1970s. Since then it has housed the innovative Fortune Theatre Company. Keep climbing, past another small terrace, Chapman's.

Take a short detour up Smith Street and walk up to two Catholic landmarks. The one closer to you, in Tennyson Street, the former St Dominic's Priory (1877) was highly experimental for its time, the largest unreinforced concrete building in the southern

Francis Petre – 'Lord Concrete' – designed both St Joseph's Cathedral (left) and the former Dominican Priory (right). Concrete was an unusual material to use for a building in 1877 and the priory was the largest unstressed, poured concrete building in the Southern Hemisphere.

hemisphere. Built for the Dominican Sisters, it was designed by architect Francis Petre, whose love of the material earned him the nickname 'Lord Concrete'. The 'unreinforced' part of its description has been a problem in recent decades. Beside it, Petre stuck to more traditional materials, Oamaru stone and local basalt. St Joseph's Catholic Cathedral has been dominating the Rattray/Tennyson Street intersection since 1886.

Once one of the country's biggest schools, the former technical school and polytechnic still dominates Upper Stuart Street.

Return to Stuart Street. Two huge educational complexes dominate Upper Stuart Street. The first, the massive brick and Oamaru stone King Edward Technical College, on the corner of Stuart Street and York Place, dates from 1913. King Edward Tech trained many famous artists and musicians. From the 1960s its tertiary component was known as the Otago Polytechnic. The Polytechnic moved down to the university campus area late last century. A couple of blocks up, in Arthur Street, off London Street, and handsomely silhouetted against the green belt, you will find the impressively spiky Port Chalmers/Oamaru stone complex of Otago Boys' High School. They are the work of our old friend Robert Lawson and were opened in 1885 to replace an earlier structure. The newer buildings are by Ted McCoy.

Set dramatically against the Town Belt, Robert Lawson's neo-Gothic Otago Boys' High tower block is a city landmark.

Backtrack a little and cross Stuart Street to continue down London Street. Before you do so, look up Stuart Street to your left. Moana Pool, by the edge of the Town Belt, is the city's Olympic swimming pool. It was the City Council's centennial project. Since it opened in 1964, Moana has turned out many New Zealand Olympic and Commonwealth Games medallists. Recent extensions have offered hydro slides and other diversions for the less competitive.

Keep going down London Street. The grander houses, on the west side of the street, are best seen from the city-side footpath, which also takes you past the entrance to the Globe Theatre, Dunedin's 'playhouse in a garden'. Enter Royal Terrace on your left. Keep to the left footpath. As you will see, Royal Terrace is part of Dunedin's 'dress circle'. There are some student flats here,

Buddhists now live and pray in Linden, 22 Royal Terrace (1878), confectioner Richard Hudson's old home.

of course, but Royal Terrace and the streets that intersect were the favoured address of Dunedin's wealthier set. Dunedin's old money crowd may have been newcomers but they built to last. Linden, 22 Royal Terrace, now the Dhargyey Buddhist Centre, dates from 1878 and from 1896 was home to biscuit baron Richard Hudson; his son, also Richard, lived at 12 Royal Terrace. The family of painter Francis Hodgkins lived at Claverton, 30 Royal Terrace, between 1878 and 1884.

But pick of the bunch is Olveston (1906), at 42 Royal Terrace. London architect Sir Ernest George designed this 35-room, Jacobean-style brick mansion covered in Moeraki pebbles and faced with Oamaru stone, for businessman David Theomin. Its magnificent interior reflects the Theomins' taste in the arts (they were prominent supporters of the art gallery) and the lifestyle of Dunedin's colonial business élite. Theomin's daughter, Dorothy, left the house to the city in 1966 and it remains one of New Zealand's most-visited historic houses. There is an admission charge; book in advance.

Take Cobden Street down past St Hilda's College and turn left into another 'dress circle' street, Heriot Row, to admire more fine houses, Leading arts and crafts architect Basil Hooper designed 26 Heriot Row (1914) for NMA and Union Company director George Ritchie. The footpath offers superb views of city and harbour as you walk north to the intersection with Pitt Street, which you should follow down, admiring more fine houses as you go.

There is no mistaking our final stop on this walk, Knox Church, on the other side of the Pitt/George Street intersection, with its 50-metre high spire. Architect Robert Lawson (who replaced sacked David Ross) insisted on that spire, tired of working on churches that ran out of funds before they could pay for their crowning glories. This one had pounds in the bank and was opened on 1876. With its blue-grey stone from the Water of Leith quarry, grey slate roofs and Oamaru stone detailing, Knox is the quintessential Dunedin Victorian building. Inside, the standout features are the great hammer-beam roof and the transept windows. In the grounds you will see a bust of Knox's minister, Dr Donald McNaughton Stuart, whose statue we saw near Queen's Gardens. He was the leader of the moderate party that watered down the Free Church's hard line on dancing, drinking and music. By 'skilfully adapting the original vision to the new demographic realities', as Erik Olssen observed, Stuart preserved the Presbyterian social influence in his city, paralleling the solidity of its architecture. In his day he was probably the most respected man in Dunedin. 'His self-abnegation and his disregard of formality were a legend', another historian noted. 'One late night he had been arrested by a newly arrived constable, carrying his own blankets through the streets to put on the bed of a sick woman'.

Sumptuously and completely furnished, Olveston (1906), one of the country's finest historic houses, attracts tens of thousands of visitors a year.

Dr Donald McNaughton Stuart, Knox's first minister, was a voice of compassion and moderation in early Dunedin.

Just round the corner from work

Knox Church, opened in 1876, is another fine example of Robert Lawson's Gothic flair.

The edge of the hospital. My hairdresser is up Albany st
Walk past here on way to work

Above: The Captain Cook Tavern is as much a part of the campus as the Registry. Some would say more so ….

Left: Dunedin artists now display their work in the old Dunedin North Post Office.

The New post office is directly opposite

Been to the coffee shop here - sells good coffee

The inviting entrance of the Otago Museum. There is a cafe inside. Otago Museum

4: North Dunedin Walk

You can choose your starting point for this walk. If you want a little liquid refreshment, you may like to fortify yourself at the spiritual heart of Scarfie Country, the Captain Cook Tavern on the corner of Albany and Great King Streets. This plain old pub replaced a wooden 1860s 'Cook' in 1873, although modifications at approximately twenty-year intervals since the 1950s have moved its interior grudgingly and austerely almost in keeping with the times. If Free Church-inclined voices are whispering in your head, you may prefer to start from the pretty little former Dunedin North Post Office building diagonally opposite. It has housed the Otago Art Society for decades. Or the University Bookshop opposite.

Walk across the museum reserve to the new Oamaru stone and glass curtain wall that capped the Otago Museum's $18 million makeover in 2000. It gave a friendly and inviting new face to what was until then four buildings connected by the architectural equivalent of a shotgun wedding: the 1877 David Ross building on Great King Street, the 1909 Hocken Wing at the Union Street end, the 1930 Fels Wing and the 1968 Centennial Wing facing the Museum Reserve. The names Hocken and Fels are steeped in Dunedin colonial history. Indeed, the museum, impressive for a city of this size, still displays many pieces given by these 'gentlemen collectors' in the days when Dunedin was our wealthiest city. You will find excellent displays of antiquities, textiles and fine arts and, at the very top of the complex, a bird gallery that manages to preserve some of the flavour of the nineteenth-century colonial collections. But other galleries are as up-to-date as you could want. Highlights include magnificent items from ancient Egypt, Greece and Rome, excellent Maori and Pacific galleries, the country's most complete collection of ship models and artefacts (honouring the Union Steam Ship Company), full natural history galleries, and the ultra-modern, 'Southern Land, Southern People'. A shop, toilets and café cater to less cerebral needs.

The space-age Information Services Building on the university campus makes striking use of a traditional building material.

The University of Otago campus is an eclectic mix of historic and state-of-the-art. The side between the Leith and the museum is probably the least interesting. The Oamaru stone pillars near the Castle Street entrance to the high-tech Information Services Building are straight out of the Flintstones – Bedrock meets Silicon Valley – but the other buildings are mostly 1960s/1970s government architecture at its blandest, redeemed perversely only by the sheer awfulness of the Hocken Building (1980). Walk northeast past the Student Union and the Hocken horror, and cross the bridge over the Leith. No river, no mere creek, this is

Left: Students compare notes during Orientation Week. Behind them banks, clubs and religious groups tout their wares from tents on the Student Union Lawn.

Below: Many student flats are adorned with names, 'appropriated' road signs and ancient furniture.

the Water of Leith. Students run bike races down it during Capping, unspeakable things get discharged into it, but somehow fish still swim in, rather than float on, the Leith. It lacks the Avon's charms, but those grey concrete prison walls are necessary. Before they were put in, the Leith had a nasty habit of flooding this part of town. And on a fine day the seats and lawns are a great place to relax.

You are now in picture-postcard Dunedin, the Registry or Clock Tower complex. Otago's Lowland Scots settlers took education seriously, educating girls more thoroughly than other British colonists. The provincial council established New Zealand's first university in 1869. When it opened in the Exchange two years later, offices and shops shut to let people watch the ceremonies. Maxwell Bury's 1879 Clock Tower Block salutes its model, the Glasgow University of 1870, with a vivid contrast of white Oamaru stone and Leith Valley basalt. The site has a harmony of style that reflects the care later architect Edmund Anscombe put into the

Opposite: Not Coronation Street … but Dundas Street, home to the city's greatest concentration of terrace housing.

extensions to the southern end in 1912 and 1922. The Geology Block (1878) and the former School of Mines (1909) show how important mining was to the economy of the day. Another adjacent Gothic block, Allen Hall (1914), was the original student centre. The Gothic campus buildings were finally completed in 1923 when builders put the finishing touches on Marama Hall, named to honour a wartime hospital ship. North of the Clock Tower complex off quiet St David Street are semi-detached Moeraki gravel-plastered brick professorial houses, Sale-Black and Scott-Shand, still named after the four founding professors.

Allen Hall, originally the student centre, is part of the harmonious precinct around the Registry.

Leave the Registry precinct by crossing the Leith by the bridge at St David Street and walk west. On your left, down Castle Street, Selwyn College and student flats remind you that you are in Scarfie Country. Some old flats feature earthy names. At times when students are shifting digs, you may find mattresses and beds burning in front of the flats. Pretend you are Desmond Morris or David Attenborough, and observe closely.

Turn left into Cumberland Street and walk north, past the modern Crown Research building to the polychromatic brick Victorian splendour of All Saints Church. Designed by W.H. Clayton, for the 'Little Enemy', the Anglicans, All Saints dates back to 1865 (chancel and transepts 1873) and is the city's oldest Anglican church. Continue north to Dundas Street, enter it and walk east. Dundas Street runs from the opulent Town Belt in the west to the damp and dank area down by Logan Park. Although gentrification is underway, students and working-class families have made their homes in places like the Dundas Street terrace houses. New Zealand colonists turned their back on terrace housing. They had seen enough of it in crowded, smoky old Britain, but Dunedin has several pockets. Ironically, modern city-dwellers now see them as attractive alternatives to villas.

Architect William Henry Clayton made the most of the brickwork when he designed All Saints Church (1865).

Yet more concrete! Castlamore, designed by 'Lord Concrete' for Judge Henry Chapman, although it was called 'Woodside' then. It is more impressive than beautiful.

If you think you have seen this before, you are right. Banker-politician William Larnach instructed architect Robert Lawson to design a scaled-down First Church as his mausoleum.

Follow Dundas Street east across the Leith bridge and up the slight rise to join Lovelock Avenue, passing more fine villas and their sometimes equally interesting denizens. The distinctive concrete house at 4 Lovelock dates from 1875 and has worn the names Woodside and Castlamore. Designed in Tudor Renaissance style but built in concrete for Judge Chapman, it is another creation of Francis Petre, 'Lord Concrete'. A few metres past it a plaque honours Olympic athlete Jack Lovelock, after whom this road was renamed.

The 17 m tall spire of Larnach's tomb announces the Northern Cemetery's presence long before you see anything else. We will get on Larnach shortly but first we must join Dunedin Rotarians in paying homage to Thomas Bracken (1843–98). Just outside the gates a large plaque features Bracken's photograph and his credentials. Walk past the 1872 Sexton's Cottage and follow the signs pointing to Bracken. You will find him almost a third of the way around the road that loops around the cemetery. Disproving the theory that size counts, Bracken's mid-sized tomb holds centre stage, appropriate enough for someone whose first collection of verse was entitled *Behind the Tomb*. It bears the text of his best-known poem, 'Not Understood'. English students have been known to gather there for poetry readings.

Of course, there is more to the Northern Cemetery than this planted poet. As you wend your way around the toppled headstones, rusted iron railings and mature plantings, you will encounter a virtual roll-call of colonial Dunedin's elite – Kempthornes, McGlashans, Somervilles, Thompsons. Be warned, some cannot help themselves even in death. Six feet under and still sanctimonious, William Thompson (died 1891) wags his finger at you, reminding you that you will share his fate. Was the old fart that insufferable in life? Just past the smug old bore is Larnach's plot. You cannot miss it. Dunedin's shakiest merchant prince paid

Thomas Bracken's last resting-place is more modest than Larnach's but probably more-visited.

Robert Lawson to design a scaled-down First Church for his mausoleum. That did not stop someone swiping his skull sixty years later, or vandals scratching their homage to Lou Reed and other newer New Iniquities. Sturdy railings now surround the mausoleum; are they there to keep lowlife out or him in?

From Bracken's Lookout you can see much of the city.

The Town Belt

Nearly forty years ago, K.C. McDonald reminded Dunedinites of the debt they owed to the people who reserved and tenaciously protected the Town Belt, running more or less contiguously along the city rise in an irregular crescent-shape.

Of course, then, as now, there was little agreement on the best use of the reserve. Some land was lopped off, people grazed cattle on it, others felled timber, roads appeared here and there, but the public-spirited largely preserved the integrity of what was called the 'city's lungs'. In the 1880s they formed the Dunedin Amenities Society to continue what the earlier indignation meetings and ad hoc protest meetings had begun. Under the watchful eye of Alexander Bathgate, the society worked alongside the council to protect and develop the Town Belt, gardens and reserves. It still does.

There are several beautiful lookouts around the Town Belt. As well as Bracken's Lookout, others include the Byrd Memorial Lookout by Unity Park (off Eglinton Road) and Queens View.

Dunedin Botanic Gardens. The rock gardens are popular on a sunny day.

As you leave the cemetery, follow the road 200 m south alongside the hedge, past the big gum trees to Bracken's Lookout for great views south over city out to ocean. Then retrace your steps. A few metres to the north of the cemetery gates follow the sealed pedestrian path that takes you straight up the hill and away from the traffic of Lovelock Avenue. Pass the big concrete tank and stop when you reach a carpark on your left. You are at the top of the Dunedin Botanic Gardens. Enter near the noticeboard.

Dunedin's public gardens are the country's oldest. They began modestly on the present site of the university in 1863. Five years later one of the Leith's pesky floods washed them away. Bowing to nature, the authorities re-established them here. There are basically two areas, the Upper and the Lower Gardens. The hilly Upper, which we are wending our way down, follows Victorian practice by setting out plants by geographical location (e.g., North Asia, North, South and Central America, the Himalayas). Here, too, you will find the aviary. Star attraction each spring, though, is the renowned Rhododendron Dell at the southern end of the Upper Garden.

The Lower Garden has a delightful rock garden (established in 1904 by Superintendent of Reserves, David Tannock), camellia, rose, herb, water and other themed gardens. Here, too, are sheltered lawns, a duck pond, playground and refreshment stops. The many fine historic features include the 1889 Wolff Harris Fountain (moved from Queen's Gardens), the 1908 Winter Garden and the 1914 band rotunda, still used on Sunday afternoons. The visitor centre/shop in the 1960s tea kiosk in the Lower Garden has leaflets on the natural and historic features of the gardens.

That concludes this walk. You can either return to the university and city along student villa-studded Castle Street (leave by the south-eastern exit), or the walking track between the trees and the Leith. If that seems too much effort, go to the exit at the North Road/Opoho gates and cross to the Gardens shopping centre, where you will find buses and taxis.

The tea kiosk (left) and the winter garden (right) peep above the shrubs and flowers of the Lower Garden.

Have been to Larnach Castle then the drive along the top road is beautiful

This is the drive out i like.

Otago Peninsula & Harbour

St Clair is the most popular of the city's southern necklace of white-sand beaches. Sharp eyes may just make out the 'shark bell' at the northern end of the Esplanade.

This is a lovely beach, popular.

Spot the Surfers!

For those not game to catch the surf outside, the pool's warm waters provide a comfortable alternative 'taste of the briny'.

Been swimming here a few times

5: Selected City Highlights

SOUTH

St Clair Beach; Cargill's Castle; and Tunnel Beach

St Clair Beach

The long sweep of the St Kilda/Middle/St Clair beaches offer some of the south's most breath-taking white sand beaches and some of its most breath-catching cold water. But since the late 1980s, the availability of cheap wetsuits and fading memories of shark attacks (Dunedin has had more than any other place in the country) have revived the popularity of surfing. St Clair, the most popular city beach, now hosts national and regional championships. The revitalisation of the Esplanade has kept locals arguing recently, but it is still a pleasant place to strut your stuff or to watch others. At the southern end is the St Clair Hot Salt Water Pool. There has been a pool at St Clair since 1884, but this complex underwent a massive redevelopment in 2001–2. The water is heated to 28 degrees Centigrade, offering bathers an alternative to what Council-speak calls the 'occasionally chilly ocean water'. It is open during the summer months, approximately from October to April. From just beyond the pool, a track leads to rocky Second Beach.

Cargill's Castle

Perched atop St Clair, and offering beautiful coastal and city views, is 'The Cliffs' or Cargill's Castle, the ruins of a 21-room mansion designed in 1876 by 'Lord Concrete' for Edward Bowes Cargill. Cargill, you will remember, denounced the 'New Iniquity'

The ruins of Cargill's Castle continue to defy developers and nature as suburbia encroaches.

but later made his peace (and his fortune) with them, sitting on the boards of the Union Company, Westport Coal, NZ Refrigerating, Mosgiel Woollens, National Insurance, Dunedin Water & Gas, Trustees Executors and the Otago & Southland Investment Company. In 1898 Dunedin elected him mayor for its fiftieth anniversary celebrations. After he died in 1901 his pretentious pile went downhill, serving at various times as a cabaret, restaurant, private home and wartime lookout. By the 1970s, however, it was just an empty shell, clinging to the hill in defiance of the elements, its own jerry-building and developers, as it still is today.

Tunnel Beach

Tunnel Beach, one of the city's most popular short walks, also has a Cargill connection. John Cargill's family had its workers dig the tunnel to give them access to this spectacular beach, with its sea stacks, arches and wind and sea-carved cliffs. On the right day the views are sensational.

Take Middleton Road and follow Blackhead Road to the signposted car park. Allow about 30 minutes down and another ten or so for the return (upward) journey.

Visitors now outnumber brewers as the popularity of brewery tours increases.

CENTRAL: FACTORY TOURS

Two inner-city manufacturers operate information centres and themed factory tours. Both charge admission and it is advisable to book ahead – contact the Dunedin Visitor Centre or the operators. Weekdays are better if you want to see the factories working.

This tap, connected to the bore beneath the brewery, is popular with Dunedinites and visitors alike, offering free water taken straight from the brewery's bore.

Speight's Heritage Centre, 200 Rattray Street

From dawn to dusk cars pull up outside the big brick brewery to fill plastic containers with free water from the Speight's bore-water tap. That water supply encouraged James Speight, Charles Greenslade and William Dawson to build their City Brewery in Rattray Street in 1876. But the business really took off under his son, Charles Speight, who made the brewery New Zealand's biggest. Speight's shipped so much beer over the Dunedin wharf that after World War One the company joined other local manufacturers in launching its own shipping line. Waterfront wags dubbed the beer-laden ship 'The Mercy Ship'. In 1923 Speight merged his brewery with others to form New Zealand Breweries.

Much of the complex dates from the mid twentieth century. A virtually new brewery was built in the late 1940s and the malt houses and other buildings on the west side of Rattray Street burned down in June 1940. Speight's experienced mixed fortunes late last century and cut back in the 1980s to concentrate on the production of draught beers only, using its own well water.

The tour takes about seventy-five minutes and concludes with some generous sampling of the sponsor's fine product.

Cadbury World, 280 Cumberland Street

The Cumberland sweet factory had its beginnings in 1868 when Richard Hudson, an unschooled orphan lured to Otago by gold, founded a biscuit bakehouse. He began humbly by hawking his ships' biscuits from a barrow on the wharves, but prospered and in 1884 started making what was claimed to be the first chocolate manufactured in the southern hemisphere. Hudson's biscuits and chocolates were a household name throughout New Zealand when the company sold out to British giant Cadbury's in 1930. Until recently known as Cadbury Schweppes Hudson Ltd, Cadbury's now concentrates on chocolates and confectionery. It is one of Dunedin's biggest factories.

NORTH

Gardens, two walks and the steepest street in the world.

Woodhaugh Gardens and the Upper Leith and Ross Creek Dam Walk

You can drive to the historic Ross Creek dam via Burma Road in Maori Hill, but it is more fun to walk through the Woodhaugh Gardens (enter near the northern end of George Street) and on up the valley. It starts gently with the lawns, shrubs and picnic areas of the gardens, which finish at Malvern Street. From there, follow the road across the bridge by the old Woodhaugh Hotel to join the Upper Leith Walkway. As you go further up the valley, signs will tell you about the flora and fauna of the area, and the boulder trap, built by city engineers to curb the Leith's destructive peregrinations. A bit further along you will pass the remains of an old stone quarry. But nature is the main star here. New Zealand pigeons, fantails and bellbirds can be seen and heard, along with introduced species. A rare remnant of kahikatea swamp forest grows along the banks of the Leith. Other native trees include matai, lowland ribbonwood and lacebark. In season, pigeons make the most of kowhai flowers and miro fruit.

Beauty and utility meet at the Boulder Trap on the Upper Leith Walk. It is part of the long battle to tame the flood-prone Water of Leith.

The track can be muddy in places and steep towards the end, but the bush and fresh air will compensate for any slight discomfort. You finally emerge from the bush by the earth banks

This at the bottom of the hill from us
Gas BBQ's for public use

of the 'Royal Albert Reservoir', as Ross Creek Reservoir was christened in 1867. The Dunedin Waterworks Company built it for the old Town Board, whose water supply, 'only fit for sewage', someone complained, could not keep up with Dunedin's booming population. The company went through three engineers but, despite occasional leaks, the reservoir worked successfully. It still does, one of just three functioning nineteenth-century water supply dams in the country. The dams – No. 1 (23m high) and No. 2 (10m) – have a puddled clay core and hold 225 million litres. You can thank the company's first engineer, Ralph Donkin, for the delightful valve tower with its alternating bands of Port Chalmers breccia and Leith Valley andesite.

Left: Woodhaugh Gardens is a popular recreation spot.

Right: The Victorian-era Ross Creek water valve tower captures the photographers' attention, but the dams are equally interesting and historic. They feature a 'puddled' clay core, i.e., clay that had been soaked and then compacted.

Been running around here

Baldwin Street

Dunedin's steepest street is also the world's steepest, with its own entry in the *Guinness Book of Records.* At its steepest the gradient is a calf-sculpting 1 in 2.86 or 19 degrees. During Festival Week runners social and serious take on the 'Baldwin Gutbuster' race to the top and back, but during other times a walk will do. Baldwin Street is in North East Valley, a short walk up from the Botanic Gardens, and is near a bus stop for your return journey.

Baldwin Street, the world's steepest street. That was about as far as the cyclist (rear) got!

Mount Cargill

Mount Cargill is Dunedin's grandest peak. It is also its moodiest. You can be soaking up the sun in George Street on the calmest of days as fog or low cloud ooze their way down its slopes, swallowing up the tall television tower and offering a passable imitation of the beard of the patriarch after whom it is named. Conversely, on another equally fine day its peak and slopes glow in the afternoon sunshine in tones of gold and brown. Always carry a change of clothing up here.

Three main routes take you to Mount Cargill. From the harbour side, a carpark on the Mount Cargill Road past the quarries offers the quickest route (about 45 minutes) to the Organ Pipes. From the top of North East Valley, an 80–90 minute hike up Bethune's Gully will lead you to a track that lets you go to either the Organ Pipes or to the Mount Cargill Road.

The easiest way is to drive from the city up Pine Hill and Cowan Roads to the carpark just a short distance below the 104.6-metre television tower (a plane table and viewing platform just past the structure serve those in a hurry). If you would like a walk, follow the signs along the A.H. Reed Memorial Track (named after the prolific Dunedin author, publisher and walker, who made an annual pilgrimage up Mount Cargill until his ninety-ninth year). It is formed for most of its length. On a fine day you can see out over Blueskin Bay, Waitati and the northern coastline and well inland.

Just past the intersection of the Reed/Organ Pipes and Bethunes tracks, a short scramble up the Buttars Peak track offers 'King of the Castle' views in all directions. After seeing your fill, return to the main track and follow it down for 20–30 minutes to the Organ Pipes, columns of upright jointed basalt rock, formed as rock cooled in the throat of the ancient Dunedin volcano. Watch your step on the lower rocks – some are very loose.

Return the way you came.

Keep an eye out for the traditional dry stone walling at the start of Cowan Road.

Right: Like something from a science fantasy movie, the Organ Pipes emerge from the mist and gloom that often caps Mount Cargill.

Below: Early morning mist clears, revealing a breath-taking panorama of the City of Dunedin.

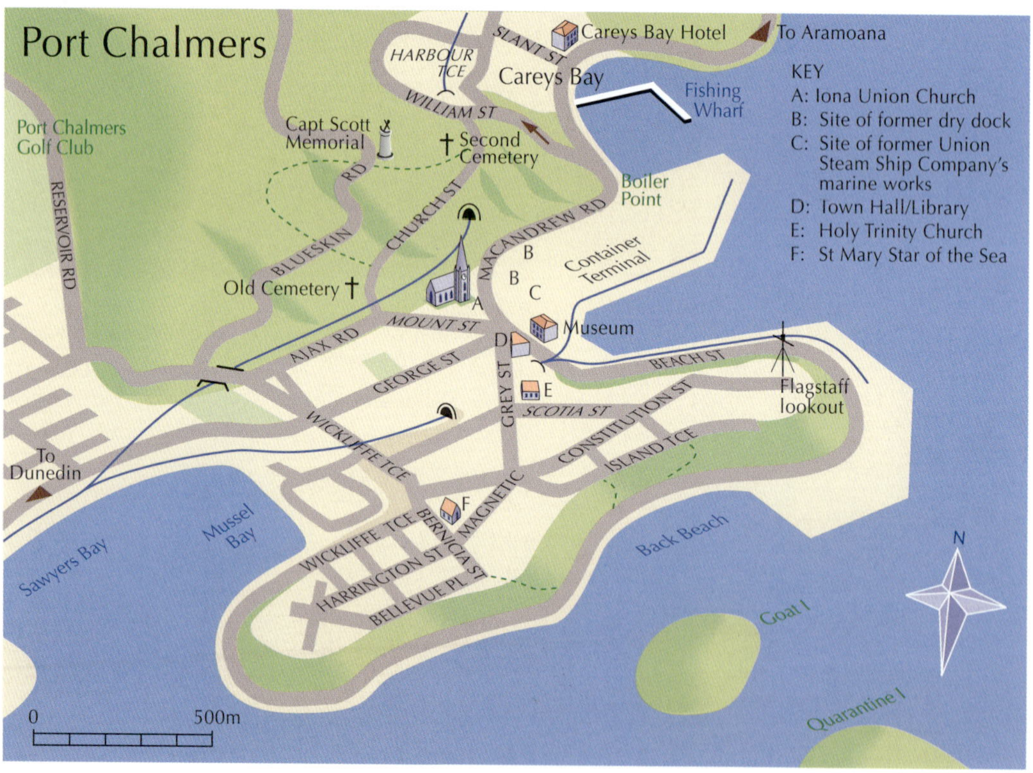

Port Chalmers
Careys Bay Hotel
To Aramoana
HARBOUR TCE
SLANT ST
Careys Bay
WILLIAM ST
Fishing Wharf
KEY
A: Iona Union Church
B: Site of former dry dock
C: Site of former Union Steam Ship Company's marine works
D: Town Hall/Library
E: Holy Trinity Church
F: St Mary Star of the Sea
Port Chalmers Golf Club
Capt Scott Memorial
Second Cemetery
RESERVOIR RD
BLUESKIN RD
CHURCH ST
MACANDREW RD
Boiler Point
Container Terminal
Old Cemetery
MOUNT ST
AJAX RD
Museum
GEORGE ST
GREY ST
BEACH ST
Flagstaff lookout
SCOTIA ST
CONSTITUTION ST
ISLAND TCE
WICKLIFFE TCE
To Dunedin
MAGNETIC
BERNICIA ST
Mussel Bay
Sawyers Bay
HARRINGTON ST
BELLEVUE PL
Back Beach
N
Goat I
Quarantine I
0
500m

6: Port Chalmers/Aramoana Drive

Follow Anzac Avenue into Ravensbourne Road, which will merge seamlessly into the busy Dunedin-Port Chalmers Road. Ravensbourne is the first of several small communities between the city and its deepwater port. Here and there old halls remind us of long defunct municipal bodies. Ravensbourne's big fertiliser works has been serving the region for over seventy years.

The Flagstaff lookout offers great views of the town and wharves. On the final leg up Scotia Street, keep your eyes on the harbour islands and Back Beach for the rare treat of a large ship 'threading the islands' (Quarantine Island left, Goat Island right). This big freighter seems almost to fill the gap and shows why pilots treat this gap carefully! Across the harbour Larnach's Castle lurks in the trees (top, right).

On your right in the water are the guideposts, green and red, of Victoria Channel, which runs from Kilgours Point to the Leith Wharf. Since 1881 this 'big ditch', as its critics called it, has brought big ships up to the city wharves. At low tide you can see the rock half-tide wall along its eastern edge that still keeps out silt. Victoria Channel cost a fortune to dredge, and infuriated Port Chalmers inhabitants, who felt that the ships should stop where the deep water ran out. For eighty years Port and City traded blows whenever bigger ships required deeper dredging. Over ninety per cent of shipping was using Victoria Channel by the late 1960s. But the switch to giant container ships in the 1970s turned the tables on Dunedin. Nevertheless, the port company still keeps the channel eight metres-deep at low water, enabling tankers, cement carriers, reefer ships and factory trawlers to use the Dunedin wharves.

The massive container cranes tower over Port Chalmers as you drop down George Street into the town. The huge berths they serve have invaded much of historic Koputai Bay and are off limits for safety reasons, but you can admire the big ships from the Flagstaff lookout. Turn right at the end of George Street, head up Grey Street and follow the signposts up the hill to the point. The first flagstaff went up here in 1864, salvaged from the mast of 'Bully' Hayes's ship *Cincinnati*; it was restored thirty years ago. From here you can admire the wharves and the harbour out to the Heads. On your way back down into town admire the view out over the log piles and warehouses of Back Beach to Goat and Quarantine Islands. Your luck is in if you see a big ship 'threading the needle', Nicol Passage, the 128-metre gap between Goat Island and the

Finger piers and drydocks added life to Port Chalmers last century. The biggest ship in this early 1920s view is a four-masted Shaw Savill & Albion 'Home boat' but most of the rest are Union Steam Ship Company vessels. Some are being refitted but a few are old craft and have been partly dismantled, ready for scuttling. Alexander Turnbull Library G-8370-1/1-

Three of Port Chalmers's heritage icons, photographed from the museum. The unusual wedge-shaped Municipal Offices (left, 1888) symbolised 'Port's' long battle for independence. It still houses local authority services, albeit for the Dunedin City Council. In the background, Iona Church's spire (1883) rises against the bush and lords it over Chicks Hotel (1876), once legendary with hard-playing blue-collar workers. The small reserve in front of the hotel is Tuckett's Corner, honouring the work of the pioneer surveyor of Otago.

Port Chalmers Peninsula, on its way up to the city wharves. Two old churches nearby are Holy Trinity Anglican (1874), on the corner of Grey and Scotia Streets and the Catholic Church of St Mary, Our Lady Star of the Sea (1878, with later additions), in Magnetic Street. In the Catholic church a ship propeller supports the altar, an anchor forms the base to the lectern and a ship's wheel adorns one wall.

The most prominent building is the Iona Union Church, 24 Mount Street. It is actually the third on the site. A small wooden building went up in 1852 and was replaced twenty years later by a stone building, now used as the church hall. Mason and Wales's soaring Gothic spire has been a Port icon since 1883.

Behind the church, steps lead up to the intersection of a road and a track by a small electricity substation. The steep, muddy track will take you up to Blueskin Road, which will take you the short distance to the Scott Memorial, which remembers Captain Robert Falcon Scott, who called here in 1901 and again in 1910 on his way to the Antarctic. Before aircraft took over from ships, Otago Harbour was an important staging post for polar explorers;

Ernest Shackleton, Richard E. Byrd and Lincoln Ellsworth all called in. Nearby a memorial honours Port Chalmers's role in loading the first frozen meat to leave New Zealand for Britain in 1882 aboard the ship *Dunedin.* The views are excellent in all directions.

If it is damp or you prefer a gentler walk, follow the road past the substation the short distance to the old cemetery, enjoying views of the wharves as you go. On your left the Lady Thorn Dell honours the wife of a long-serving Port mayor. On the cliffs above the shrubs fading ships' names are painted on the rock. In the days of long port stays, crews climbed up here to leave their mark. *Chakrata, Hauraki, Aotea* and other names speak from a vanished past. Ships no longer spend enough time in port for such hijinks, nor one suspects do people have much enthusiasm for monikers like *P&O Nedlloyd New Orleans.*

At the beautiful old cemetery there are historic graves and some superb views over Careys Bay to the sea. You can retrace your steps back to Iona or follow the track down to Harbour Terrace and then down the short track that comes out near the fishing wharves.

Opposite: In a port town even the church fittings sometimes take on a nautical air. At St Mary Star of the Sea Church an anchor from the old trawler Bravo *supports the lectern.*

As its no-nonsense looks suggest, the recently restored Careys Bay Hotel (ex Crescent, 1875) was built for the owner of Chicks, Henry Dench. Careys Bay, just minutes' walk from the container terminal, is an idyllic little watering hole.

George Street and thereabouts contain many prominent hotels, banks and office buildings, a throwback to the days when hundreds of watersiders, sailors and shipwrights kept the port busy. Artists' studios and craft shops rule the roost these days. The more interesting pubs include the Port Chalmers ('the Tunnel Hotel'), built on the site of the pre-1848 whare, John Anderson's 'Surveyors' Arms', and Chicks Hotel (1876), a legendary dive. The Port Chalmers Museum, housed near the entrance to the container terminal in W.H. Clayton's 1877 post office, is open weekend afternoons and other times by arrangement.

Macandrew Road peels off around George Street to skirt round the back of the container stacks where the Union Company had

Opposite: From the old cemetery you can see right out to the Heads.

its marine repair works for a century. Two big dry docks, opened in 1872 and 1909, are now entombed beneath the container terminal (though their old pump house survives). At Boiler Point (near the terminal) Stephenson & Cook built steel minesweepers in 1941–5. Wooden boat specialists Miller & Tunnage keep shipbuilding going in Careys Bay (named after David Carey, an early lighterman), which reeks as much of history as fish. Its fishing wharves are modern but they and the boats they serve have a reassuringly human scale. The old bluestone hotel has been there since 1874, when it was the Crescent. It was refurbished recently and since 2002 has been home to *Vive Aramoana*, a Ralph Hotere painting celebrating the tidal flats we shall visit shortly. In the shallows around Goldies Point and Athfields Point are traces of the hulks of sailing ships such as the *Prince Alfred* and the *Moa*, the 1867 wooden floating dock *Alpha* and William Isbister's 1864 patent slip.

The graving docks and the finger piers have gone but shipping remains Port Chalmers's lifeblood. This view out over the container terminal shows a 70,000-tonne cruise ship, the Legend of the Seas, *berthed incongruously against the Beach Street forestry berth. Flagstaff Lookout's signal mast rises above the raised boom of the right container crane.*

Macandrew Road will wind its way pleasantly out to Aramoana, do-se-doing with the shipping channel, taking you around striking rock wall-lined beaches and promontories, Hotere country if ever there was! Names like Acheron Head (named for the 1840s survey ship HMS *Acheron*) and Pulling Point (supposedly named because boatmen complaining about the strong current were told 'pull and be damned!') reinforce the place's maritime past. More tangible reminders lie in the shallows at Deborah Bay, the rotting hulks of the old sailing ships *Don Juan*, *Esk* and *California*.

As you near the harbour entrance, you pass the Aramoana salt marshes. One of the mainland's largest, they are now fully protected and are home to an extraordinary variety of plants, marine life and birds, freshened twice daily in the middle and lower zones by nutrient-rich tidal waters. At low tide they can seem crowded with seabirds – pied oystercatchers, banded dotterels, red-billed and southern black-backed gulls, pied stilts, white

Have driven out here but prefer the other side of peninsula

The road out to Aramoana features many picturesque bends and, of course, the ever-present rock walling.

herons, not to mention those summer migrants, the eastern bar-tailed godwits.

The road into the Spit near the harbour entrance takes you through the small holiday township of Aramoana ('Pathway to the Sea'). These isolated little cribs (baches to northerners) are idyllic on a sunny day and it is hard to realise that Aramoana twice made the news for all the wrong reasons late last century. In the early 1980s the 'Save Aramoana Campaign' fought the government, the harbour board and industry's plans for an aluminium smelter beside the environmentally sensitive salt marshes. Then on 13 November 1990, in New Zealand's worst mass killing, paranoid loner David Gray shot 13 people before killing himself.

The crumbling remains of the old railway staging used to build and maintain the Mole now frame excellent views of Taiaroa Head across the harbour. The afternoon sun is highlighting the lighthouse (left) and the albatross observatory (right upper).

Follow the road out to the Mole. To your left stretch the white sandy beaches of the inner arm of the Spit, where the harbour pilots were stationed for many years last century. The Mole was built in 1884–8 to the design of British marine engineer Sir John Coode. It still concentrates the scour at the entrance and keeps silt out of the channel. Fragments of the raised railway staging once used to build it add interest to the inner side. Last century redundant ships were scuttled alongside to offer additional protection and they now make the site popular with divers. Mere pedestrians like us have to be satisfied with the sight of the *Mokoia*'s sternpost poking above the water. The Mole is still a fine place to see ships coming or going, or simply just sit out at the pilot zone, about five nautical miles off shore. Taiaroa Head looks a million dollars in the afternoon sunshine and even this place has plenty of wildlife. Sea lions sun themselves on the rocks near the end and you will see terns, gulls and shags.

The Spit, seen from Pilots Beach across the harbour entrance, looking back towards Port Chalmers.

The Rongo rock commemorates Maori prisoners of war.

Prison labour – European as well as Maori – built the historic seawall.

7: Peninsula Drive

With its distinctive hills, bays and beaches, Otago Peninsula is deceptively large, about 30 km driving distance from the city centre to Taiaroa Head, and over 6 km across in places. Allow half a day to get around its harbour trail, more if you are exploring the paid attractions or the rugged Pacific Ocean inlets.

This drive will highlight the inner harbour star attractions. For more information on the peninsula's many side roads, walking and mountain biking tracks and other attractions, see the Visitor Centre, the guides on page 64, or surf the Council's website, http://www.cityofdunedin.com

You can drive or cycle out to the Peninsula. Suburban bus services go to Portobello several times a day. But tens of thousands of people take a tour. Operators offer the choice of launch (above), bus, 4-wheel drive, amphibious vehicle and mountain biking options. Ask the Visitor Centre which of the many options best suits your schedule, interests and wallet and how to mix and match attractions.

Follow Portsmouth Drive to Anderson's Bay. By the corner of Shore Street and Portobello Road, just before you reach the causeway, on your right you will see a memorial. 'Rongo' is one-tonne of rock that bears the weight of many times that amount of history. It was unveiled in March 1987 by Governor-General Sir Paul Reeves to commemorate the sufferings of the Taranaki Maori prisoners who were held in the city in 1869–72 and 1879–81. The first prisoners were put on public works around Dunedin, such as the seawalls. Most stayed in the old gaol or aboard a hulk, but some had to shelter in the Puketahi Caves at night.

It pays not to rush the long, winding road, even in fine weather, for there is much to savour, including that old seawall, built with so much sweat and pain. The narrow, winding road has never been a speed track and until the 1920s most of the Peninsula bays had their own ferry jetties. Few survive, but from time to time you will come across small clusters of boatsheds, jaunty survivors only grudgingly tolerated by bureaucrats. The small beaches are also picturesque. At certain times in summer they are bright pink/red with the bodies of trillions of red lobster krill (*munida gregaria*, commonly called whalefeed).

Glenfalloch Woodland Gardens, with its chalet and 1870s homestead, is open to the public and run by the Otago Peninsula Trust, which manages several properties. Entry is by donation. The next major bays, Macandrew Bay and Broad Bay, are attractive stopping places. Macandrew Bay, named after the colourful nineteenth-century provincial politician, James Macandrew, has a particularly good microclimate. At 727 Portobello Road, Broad Bay, you will find a little house associated with another famous James, Sir James Fletcher, who founded the Fletcher Challenge business empire. In 1909, long before his knighthood, he built this little bay window villa with the help of Albert Morris. The company has restored and furnished it to Edwardian style, offering an interesting contrast to Dunedin's grander piles. There is an

Fletcher House at Broad Bay is a restored Edwardian villa.

entry fee. Phone ahead for seasonal opening times.

Portobello, once known as Limeburners' Bay, about twenty-five minutes' drive from the city, is one of the larger settlements, famous for its 1874 pub and the marine aquarium, 2 km along Hatchery Road. The road's name commemorates the old Portobello Fish Hatchery, which the university took over in 1951. Otago has New Zealand's only Department of Marine Science. Here staff and students research southern marine life. In 1997 the university complex was joined by the New Zealand Marine Studies Centre, a modern visitor attraction, complete with 'touch tank' and ever-changing displays. It is open in the afternoons (admission charges apply). There is also the Otago Peninsula Museum (open Sunday afternoons). From the Portobello Peninsula, the largest component of the Portobello-Quarantine-Goat-Port Chalmers barrier that divides the Lower and Upper Harbours, you get the best views of Quarantine Island (also sometimes known as St Martin's Island, because of its associations with a religious community). The island has an old migrant-era

The modern aquarium has taken over from the old fish hatchery. Quarantine Island is in the background.

The main buildings and structures at Otakou Marae were completed between 1940 and 1946, although the old kaika's history is far longer than that.

building, a World War One hospital building, and two hulks, the more prominent being the harbour ferry *Waikana*. In keeping with Victorian propriety, Quarantine Island housed married couples, single women and children, while the single men camped a chaste distance away on Goat Island. The small island near Portobello is Pudding Island.

We are now about fifteen minutes from Taiaroa Head. A short distance past the Otakou fishing wharf, take Tamatea Road on your right up to the Otakou Marae and church. This part of the harbour is rich in history. Otakou is still the heartland of Dunedin Kai Tahu. The 1941 brick church, covered with a Moeraki gravel finish, has concrete decorative panels that look like wood from a distance. Like the centennial gate (1940), it commemorated two major events of 1840, the establishment of the first Christian mission in the South Island by the Rev. James Watson, and the signing of the Treaty of Waitangi. Tamatea meetinghouse was completed in 1946. In the cemetery lie important leaders such as Karetai and Te Matenga Taiaroa. The church museum can be seen by arrangement; phone beforehand. Back at the harbour's edge, on the promontory a short distance past the marae turnoff, Weller's Rock bears a memorial plaque to the whaling station established here in 1831. Iron bars from the whaling era still jut from the rock; the newer jetty is used by the wildlife cruise launch. Nearby is a memorial to Catholic Bishop Pompallier, who said Mass on 22 November 1840.

An iron spike thrust into Weller's Rock is a reminder of its early role as a whaling station.

Continue on to Taiaroa Head. The pretty beach in its lee is Pilots' Beach, a sheltered swimming and picnic spot. From here harbour pilots once set off in all weathers, pulling on the oars of their open boats. These days the only residents are the sea lions on the beach, the fur seals on the rocks and the little blue penguins, which can be seen at the reserve at the northern end of the beach.

This fur seal is enjoying the sunshine at the rocky end of Pilots Beach.

Majestic Taiaroa Head dominates the approaches to the harbour entrance, so it is not surprising that it has a long history. Pukekura Pa was occupied long before the Europeans arrived, one of Otago's few defended headland pa. It was destroyed by nineteenth-century fort-building. From the 1880s until World War Two, large guns defended Otago Harbour. There were several sites in and around the Peninsula. A smaller complex can be seen below the 'Fortifications' sign at Harington Point about 1 km before Taiaroa Heads, for example. But Taiaroa Head was the key, where the

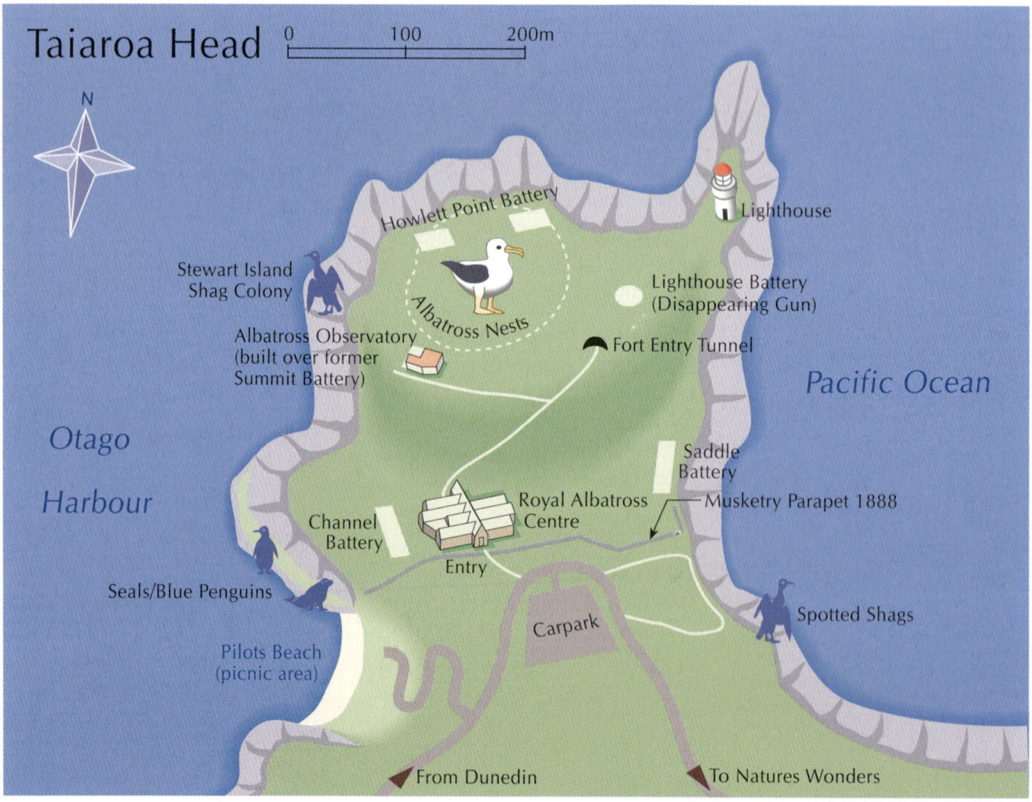

Taiaroa Head's dramatic rock cliffs provide attract many seabirds. Further down, seals and penguins make the most of the water and the rocks.

Lighthouse Battery was one of half a dozen batteries built during the 1880s Russian war scares. Mounted on a hydro-pneumatic carriage, its Armstrong 6-inch (152-mm) disappearing gun was aimed while underground, then raised, fired and returned back to the pit by the recoil for reloading: Victorian 'stealth' technology! Thirty years ago volunteers restored it to working order. Access is via the modern Royal Albatross Centre. Casual visitors can view the centre's displays on Maori, military and maritime history but, as with most Peninsula attractions, book in advance if you want to see the disappearing gun or get close to the albatrosses. The Summit Battery has been destroyed, as has much of the Channel Battery, whose few remains are, like the largely intact Howlett Battery, now off-limits behind the albatross colony fences. Until very recently, you had free access to the substantial concrete remains of the Saddle Battery, on the eastern side. Historic heritage comes a very poor second here.

Port functions have dominated Taiaroa Head ever since the first flagstaff went up in 1849. Pilots, signalmen and others lived here for decades, joined later by the gunners. By the 1890s the 100 residents had a schoolteacher, deliveries of meat and groceries twice weekly and regular visits from the draper. How different to now! The port company closed the signal station recently and now monitors things from Port Chalmers by remote control. Also automated is the point's heritage showpiece, the 1864 lighthouse, built by Hugh Calder from locally quarried stone for just £3,150.

The warriors and mariners have left Taiaroa Head to Department of Conservation staff and tourism operators at this internationally significant ecotourism destination. Top of the bill, in every sense of the phrase, are the royal albatross, or toroa. These are actually something of a cuckoo in the nest, since the present colony, the only mainland royal albatross one in the world, dates

Had coffee in Cafe here

from the 1930s. It is the doing of teacher and ornithologist Lance Richdale, who with magnificent obsession (often spending long hours camped out protecting the nests), made the colony a success. With their wingspan of about three metres, Dunedin's royals are a magnificent sight as they glide in to land. Parents incubate the eggs for 80 days or so from November, males and females taking turns. When the chicks take to the air the following year, they begin an odyssey that may keep them away for three or four years.

But there is more to see than albatross. *Time* magazine described Richdale as 'the Kinsey of the penguin world', and in and around Taiaroa Head you will find both the world's smallest penguin, the very common blue (korara) and the rare and endangered yellow-eyed (hoiho) penguin. Several tours can take you penguin-spotting. Other seabirds congregating hereabouts include spotted, Stewart Island and little shags, southern black-backed and red-billed gulls, white-fronted terns, oystercatchers and sooty shearwaters.

When you have seen enough of albatrosses and artillery, drive back along the harbour road. If you are in a hurry, follow it right back to Company Bay, turn into Castlewood Road, and head up to the signs that will direct you to Larnach's Castle. Otherwise, take Weir's Road, about halfway between Harwood and Portobello. It is a longer, slower route, but in fine weather it offers magnificent views of the Peninsula's rugged Pacific coast. Sheppard Road will take you along the edge of Papanui Road and on around Hoopers Inlet via the road of that name. If you have time, you can wind your way out to the Peninsula's other large lighthouse, Cape Saunders. Otherwise, follow Sandymount Road (keep an eye out for the distinctive 1865 lime kiln) around to Highcliff Road, which will bring you to Pukehiki (q.v.). From Pukehiki, Camp Road will lead you up the short distance to the turnoff to Larnach's Castle.

Top: A royal albatross glides past the lighthouse.

Bottom: Visitors to the yellow-eyed penguin colony can usually expect to get very close to the birds.

Originally called 'The Camp' by its owner, this 43-roomed Scots baronial house symbolised the wealth and confidence of the Dunedin business community at its peak. Work started on the isolated Otago Peninsula in 1871, supervised by architect Robert Lawson. It is an impressive if clumsy mixture of colonial Victorian and Scottish styles. It was also expensive. Sculptor Louis Godfrey and others created magic with the stone, wood and plaster work. Although Larnach moved in in 1874, work on the interior continued for many years, and the ballroom was not completed until 1887. The family did not enjoy it for long. Larnach speculated, borrowed and lived life close to the edge. So did his son, who took up with his father's third wife while living here. Soon after Larnach's dramatic suicide at Parliament in 1898, the house passed from family hands, experiencing many ups and downs. At one stage sheep were kept in the ruined ballroom. Since 1967 the Barker family has slowly and painfully restored the house, outbuildings and beautiful grounds to a major attraction. The view from the battlements is superb. The ornate cupola in the grounds is reputed to have been salvaged from the Union Company steamer *Zealandia*. There is an admission charge, but casual visitors are welcome.

After leaving the Castle, follow Camp Road down to where it joins Highcliff Road at Pukehiki. Note the 1868 Pukehiki Community Church and the delightful little library. In 1871 nearby, John Mathieson from 'Springvale', and neighbours built the country's first co-operative cheese factory. There is a memorial plaque and 'Springvale' homestead still stands. Also around this part of the Peninsula are the distinctive dry-stone walls, built by the early settlers. As you make your way down to the city you will pass the Soldiers' Memorial Lookout; on a clear day the short hike up the hillside offers beautiful views of the city and harbour on one side, and Tomahawk Lagoon and the Pacific on the other. Less than a kilometre along Highcliff Road, Rotary Park looks out over the harbour, city and hills. When you have gazed your fill, follow the road down to the city.

Above: Carved lions guard the castle's main entrance. They are a pun on Larnach's motto 'sans peur'.

Right: Larnach's Castle is one of the city's major tourist icons.

Been here lovely garden + breathtaking views

Tours, guides and bookings

Remember that many of the more popular attractions must be booked in advance. See the Dunedin Visitor Centre in the Octagon (phone 03 474-3300, email visitor.centre@dcc.govt.nz) for advice about seasonal opening hours, closures and other matters. It is open every day. You can also find it on the incredibly comprehensive Dunedin City Council website, http://www.cityofdunedin.com

Who pinched Plato's Pajero? St Joseph's Cathedral (1886) and the former Dominican Priory (1877) can be seen above the lawyers' car park in Smith Street, where philosophers' names replace registration numbers.

FURTHER READING

Dunedin has a long tradition of regional and local publishing. Otago Heritage Books has been the most prolific, publishing many monographs on local history, heritage and flora. Here are a few of the more general volumes.

1. Guides

Bishop, Graham and Antony Hamel, *From Sea to Silverpeaks: a Guide to the Walking Tracks, Beaches, Viewpoints and Special Attractions of Dunedin*, Silver Peaks Press, Dunedin, 4th edition, 2002

Galer, Lois, *Houses of Dunedin: An Illustrated Collection of the City's Historic Homes*, Hyndman Publishing, Dunedin, 1995

Haywood, Paul, *Intriguing Dunedin Street Walks*, *More Intriguing Dunedin Street Walks*, *Even More Intriguing Dunedin Street Walks*, *Further Intriguing Dunedin Street Walks* and *Still More Intriguing Dunedin Street Walks*, author, Dunedin. These are in the Public Library.

Knight, Hardwicke, *Church Building in Otago*, author, Dunedin, 1993

Knight, Hardwick and Niel Wales, *Buildings of Dunedin: An Illustrated Guide to New Zealand's Victorian City*, John McIndoe, Dunedin, 1988

Peat, Neville and Brian Patrick, *Wild Dunedin*, University of Otago Press, Dunedin, 2nd edition, 2002

2. History

Goodall, Maarire and George Griffiths, *Maori Dunedin*, Otago Heritage Books, Dunedin, 1980

Johnson, David, *Dunedin: A Pictorial History*, Canterbury University Press, Christchurch, 1993

McLean, Gavin, *Otago Harbour: Currents of Controversy*, Otago Harbour Board, Dunedin, 1985

Olssen, Erik, *A History of Otago*, John McIndoe, Dunedin, 1984

'Southern Man', an Auckland-run brewery's misconception of southern masculinity, greets visitors to Momona airport.